Reading from the
Bookshelf

LEVEL TWO

with questions for talk and writing

Alan Josephs

Oliver & Boyd

Introduction

Reading from the Bookshelf consists of a series of six books for the 7–12 age range. Each book contains extracts from a selection of Puffin story or picture books, almost all of which will be found to correspond to the titles chosen for the *Puffin Library Bookshelf* series produced by Oliver and Boyd. As well as the extracts, *Reading from the Bookshelf* contains follow-up reading, talk and writing activities. The series can thus be used in association with the *Library Bookshelves* or as independent text-book material. The *main* emphasis is always to excite interest in the original books.

The *Starter* Level provides picture extracts, with a limited amount of text and a few simple questions. Each unit in Levels 1–5 offers the following basic pattern:

1. an introduction to the extract;
2. an extract that has a self-contained element but is intended to stimulate interest in the book itself;
3. five basic comprehension questions (Key points);
4. a question to test deeper understanding and extended reading skills (A closer look);
5. opportunities for talk/discussion related to the extract (For talk, For discussion);
6. follow-up writing tasks (For writing);
7. an 'appetiser' related to the stage the story has reached (Read on).

In each book five of the twenty-five units provide more extensive opportunities, with a longer passage, an associated picture and poem, and questions testing wider study skills.

Oliver & Boyd
Longman House
Burnt Mill
Harlow
Essex CM20 2JE

An Imprint of Longman Group UK Ltd

First published 1986
Seventh impression 1993
ISBN 0 05 003963 6
© Oliver & Boyd 1986. The acknowledgments on page 64 constitute an extension of this copyright line.

Produced by Longman Singapore Publishers Pte Ltd
Printed in Singapore
SWT/06

The publisher's policy is to use paper manufactured from sustainable forests.

Contents

1. The cat that grew

Mrs Jones bakes bread to sell in her shop. Mog, her cat, has to keep out of the way when she is baking. One day he has been out in the rain and has come home very wet.

As Mog sat by the fire he sneezed nine times.

Mrs Jones said, 'Oh dear, Mog, are you catching a cold?'

She dried him with a towel and gave him some warm milk with yeast in it. Yeast is good for people when they are poorly.

Then she left him sitting in front of the fire and began making jam tarts. When she had put the tarts in the oven she went out shopping, taking her umbrella.

But what do you think was happening to Mog?

The yeast was making him rise.

As he sat dozing in front of the lovely warm fire he was growing bigger and bigger.

First he grew as big as a sheep.

Then he grew as big as a donkey.

Then he grew as big as a cart-horse.

Then he grew as big as a hippopotamus.

By now he was too big for Mrs Jones's little kitchen, but he was *far* too big to get through the door. He just burst the walls.

When Mrs Jones came home with her shopping-bag and her umbrella she cried out,

'Mercy me, what is happening to my house?'

The whole house was bulging. It was swaying. Huge whiskers were poking out of the kitchen window. A marmalade-coloured tail came out of the door. A white paw came out of one bedroom window, and an ear with a white fringe out of the other.

Key points

1. Why was Mrs Jones worried about Mog?
2. Why did she put yeast in his milk?
3. What mistake did Mrs Jones make?
4. Where was Mrs Jones when Mog began to change?
5. What had happened to Mrs Jones's house when she came back home?

A closer look

The yeast made Mog grow from a normal cat to one as big as a house. Make a list of the *six* stages of his growth.

For talk

Talk about the times when *you* have had a cold, and what you have been given to make you better.

For writing

What do you think happened next to Mog and Mrs Jones and her house? Write your own ending to the story.

Read on

What really happened to Mog and Mrs Jones? You can find out by reading *The Baker's Cat*, one of eight stories by Joan Aiken in her book *A Necklace of Raindrops and other stories*.

2. The hungry little owl

Plop is trying to learn to like the dark. As barn owls usually hunt at night and sleep during the day, Plop's mother and father wish he would learn quickly.

Plop, having slept nearly all day, was very lively that evening – very lively and very hungry. He kept wobbling along the branch to where his father was roosting to see if by chance he were awake and ready to go hunting.

Mr Barn Owl was drawn up tall and still. He seemed hardly to be breathing. Plop stretched up on tiptoe and tried to see into his father's face. What a strong, curved beak he had.

'Daddy, are you awake?' he said loudly. 'I'm hungry.'

Mr Barn Owl did not open his eyes, but the beak moved.

'Go away!' it said. 'I'm asleep.'

Plop went away obediently – and then realised something and went back again. 'Daddy! You can't be asleep. You spoke – I heard you.'

'You must have imagined it,' said his father, still not opening his eyes.

'You spoke,' said Plop. 'You're awake, so you can go hunting.' He butted his father's tummy with his head. 'Come on! It's getting-up time!'

Mr Barn Owl sighed and stretched. 'All right, all right, you horrible owlet. What time is it?' He looked up at the sky. 'Suffering bats! It isn't even dark yet! I could have had another half hour.' He glared at Plop. 'Dash it, I'm going to have another half hour. I will not be bullied by an addled little – little DAYBIRD. Go away! You may wake me when it is dark, and not before, d'you understand?' He suddenly leaned forward until his huge beak was level with Plop's own little carpet tack. Plop could see two of himself reflected in his father's eyes.

'Er – yes, Daddy,' he said, backing away hurriedly.

'Good,' said his father, drawing himself up to sleep again.   'Good day.'

Key points

1.   Why did Plop want his father to wake up?
2.   Why did Plop go away when he was told and *then* come back?
3.   Why did Mr Barn Owl look up at the sky?
4.   Why do you think Mr Barn Owl called Plop a DAYBIRD?
5.   What made Plop decide to leave his father alone?

A closer look

Plop was trying to wake his father up, just as a little boy or girl might do in the morning.   Make a list of the ways the two owls seemed to behave like a father and his small child.

For talk

Like Plop many children wake up earlier than their parents.   Talk about what you do when you wake up early and the rest of the house is quiet.

For writing

Mr Barn Owl did not like being nagged when he wanted to sleep.   Think of a time when you were nagging your father or mother.   Write down the conversation that took place.

Read on

Plop has to learn to go hunting at night.   Find out how he overcomes his fears when you read *The Owl who was Afraid of the Dark* by Jill Tomlinson.

3. A garden to explore

Joseph has been told that a big house near his home has a magic garden. One day the postman asks him to take some letters up the drive to the house. He gives the letters to the old lady who lives there.

The old lady did not seem in a hurry to close the door. She just stood looking out at the garden and nodding her head at something that pleased her.

'I think you have a very nice garden,' said Joseph. 'Sometimes I look at it through the fence, but I have never been inside before.'

'Have you a garden of your own?'

'Yes. It's pretty. It has Sweet Williams and a sundial. But you can cross it in five hops. I mean, I can.'

'I don't hop much,' said the old lady.

Joseph laughed, and then frowned instead of blushing. 'Our garden is not very interesting. You get used to it too soon.'

'Ah, yes. Five hops don't take you far. Now this garden is like a long book. You never know what you will find on the other side of the page. Would you like to explore it?'

'Yes, please. May I?'

'You may.'

'Can I go wherever I like?'

'You can go anywhere you want, if you really want to.'

This had a slightly solemn sound, and Joseph hesitated.

'Is there anything dangerous?' he asked.

'Go on with you,' said the old lady. 'And find out.' She closed the door.

Key points

1. Why do you think the old lady looked so pleased?
2. What was Joseph's own garden like?
3. Why did the old lady say her garden was like a long book?
4. Why did Joseph hesitate when the old lady said he could explore?
5. Why do you think the old lady closed her door?

A closer look

Imagine Joseph told his mother about the old lady and what she told him about her garden.   Write down what he said to his mother.

For talk

Talk about what you like (and dislike) about gardens and gardening.

For writing

The next line of the story begins, 'The first thing to explore was ......' Continue the story, describing where Joseph began to explore and what he found.

Read on

What *does* Joseph find in the old lady's garden?   There are many surprises and even a few dangers.   You can find out what they are in *The Castle of Yew* by Lucy Boston.

4. A greedy wolf

Polly leads a quiet life at home.   Nothing ever happens until ...

One day Polly was alone downstairs.   Camilla was using the Hoover upstairs, so when the front door bell rang, Polly went to open the door.   There was a great black wolf!   He put his foot inside the door and said:

'Now I'm going to eat you up!'

'Oh no, please,' said Polly.   'I don't want to be eaten up.'

'Oh yes,' said the wolf, 'I am going to eat you.   But first tell me, what is that delicious smell?'

'Come down to the kitchen,' said Polly, 'and I will show you.'

She led the wolf down to the kitchen.   There on the table was a delicious-looking pie.

'Have a slice?' said Polly.   The wolf's mouth watered, and he said, 'Yes, please!'   Polly cut him a big piece. When he had eaten it, the wolf asked for another, and then for another.

'Now,' said Polly, after the third helping, 'what about me?'

'Sorry,' said the wolf, 'I'm too full of pie.   I'll come back another day to deal with you.'

A week later Polly was alone again, and again the bell rang. Polly ran to open the door. There was the wolf again.

'This time I'm really going to eat you up, Polly,' said the wolf.

'All right,' said Polly, 'but first, just smell.'

The wolf took a long breath.   'Delicious!' he said. 'What is it?'

'Come down and see,' said Polly.

In the kitchen was a large chocolate cake.

'Have a slice?' said Polly.

'Yes,' said the wolf greedily.   He ate six big slices.

'Now, what about me?' said Polly.

'Sorry,' said the wolf, 'I just haven't got room.   I'll come back.'   He slunk out of the back door.

Key points

1. How did the wolf get inside the house?
2. On both visits what stopped the wolf eating Polly in the doorway?
3. On both visits what stopped the wolf eating Polly in the kitchen?
4. How had Polly tricked the wolf?
5. What did the last sentence of the passage tell you about the wolf?

A closer look

Polly was clever and the wolf was stupid.   Write down all the ways this was shown to be true in the passage.

For talk

The wolf was fond of pie and chocolate cake, and was *very* greedy. Talk about times when *you* have been greedy and what happened to you.

For writing

The passage described two visits by the wolf to Polly's house. Write a story about his next visit, beginning, 'A week later ......'

Read on

You have read about the first two of the many attempts by the wolf to catch and eat Polly.   You can read about more of them in *Clever Polly and the Stupid Wolf* by Catherine Storr.

5. Counting dragons

It is a hot summer's night. Ben and Beth cannot get to sleep and their father tells them to count sheep jumping over a gate. Beth does so and soon dozes off, but Ben decides to count dragons instead!

'Sixty-one, sixty-two', counted Ben, and then he yawned. 'I think I'm getting sleepy!' he said to himself. Aloud to Beth he went on: 'I say, it's a funny thing –' he yawned again and snuggled down under the bedclothes, 'but the sleepier I grow the smaller the dragons seem to get!'

But there was no answer from Beth. She was asleep already; the blue flowery bedspread moved very slightly up and down with her even breathing.

'Eighty-eight, eighty-nine,' counted Ben sleepily.

Now when he reached dragon ninety-eight he was almost asleep, and dragon ninety-nine was very small indeed; not much bigger than a kitten. But it clapped its flippers together bravely, as the others had done, blew a couple of sparks and a tiny thread of smoke through its nostrils, and jumped with a 'Whoops!' which was little more than a squeak. But instead of sailing over the gate as its companions had done, it stumbled against one of the golden curlicues on top of the great high gate, and fell back, plop! right on to the middle of Ben's bed, with a sad little 'Wheee!' and a slight smell of singeing.

Ben shot up in bed, very wide awake all at once. He stared at the little dragon over the hump of his knees, and the little dragon stared back, and I don't know which of them was the more surprised.

There was a long pause, and then Ben said:

'Hadn't you better go after the others?'

'How can I?' said Dragon Ninety-nine. 'That great iron gate is too high for me to jump over. They've all gone without me. Whatever shall I do?'

To Ben's horror two tears welled up from its slanting golden eyes, and trickled down its long green nose, to dry with a sizzle when they reached its smoking nostrils. 'Even if I could get over the gate I should never catch up with the others, not with my short legs. They're all bigger than me,' it went on unhappily.

Ben leaned over and shook Beth by the shoulder.

'Wake up! Wake up!' he said. 'Something awful's happened!'

'What's the matter?' said Beth, sleepily rubbing her eyes. But when she saw the little dragon she sat up at once.

'Whatever's that?' she said.

'I'm not a that, I'm a dragon!' it said sulkily, and the tears began to run down its long nose faster than ever, so that it almost disappeared in the cloud of steam they made.

Key points

1. How did Dragon Ninety-nine get its name?
2. Why did the dragons begin to get smaller as Ben went on counting?
3. How did Dragon Ninety-nine end up on Ben's bed?
4. Why did the dragon start to cry?
5. What did Beth do that upset the dragon?

A closer look

Each sentence is about Dragon Ninety-nine.   Choose what you
think is the best word for each gap.   When you have finished,
look at the passage again to see if you want to change any of
your words.

1. Dragon Ninety-nine was very small, not much bigger than a ——.
2. Its nose was long and coloured ——.
3. It had slanting eyes that were —— in colour.
4. When it tried to jump over the gate, it clapped its —— together.
5. It also blew —— through its nostrils.
6. It tried to shout 'Whoops!' but only a —— came out.
7. Instead of jumping over the gate it —— the top of it.
8. It —— right in the middle of Ben's bed.
9. There was a slight smell of ——.
10. When Dragon Ninety-nine saw Ben it was very ——.
11. It was also very ——, because the other dragons had gone without it.
12. Even if it had jumped over the gate its legs were too —— to
    keep up with the others.
13. The dragon was —— when Beth said, 'Whatever's that?'
14. It became —— and began to cry.
15. The tears turned into ——, when they reached the dragon's nostrils.

For talk

Talk about bedtime and what *you* do if you find it hard to go to sleep.

THE WENDIGO

The Wendigo,
The Wendigo!
Its eyes are ice and indigo!
Its blood is rank and yellowish!
Its voice is hoarse and bellowish!
Its tentacles are slithery,
And scummy,
Slimy,
Leathery!
Its lips are hungry blubbery,
And smacky,
Sucky,
Rubbery!
The Wendigo,
The Wendigo!
I saw it just a friend ago!
Last night it lurked in Canada;
Tonight, on your veranada!
As you are lolling hammockwise
It contemplates you stomachwise.
You loll,
It contemplates,
It lollops.
The rest is merely gulps and gollops.

Ogden Nash

For writing

Dragons are supposed to be fierce and more like the Wendigo in
the poem than Dragon Ninety-nine.   Make up a fierce creature of
your own and write a story about its visit to one of *your* dreams.

Read on

Ben and Beth want to help Dragon Ninety-nine.   You can find out how
they do so, and also how Beth's sheep and the other ninety-eight dragons
become involved, when you read *Ninety-nine Dragons* by Barbara Sleigh.

6. The crafty fox

Danny Fox has tried to steal some fish from a fisherman who is bringing his catch back to town. The fisherman is too quick for him and chases Danny off his cart and over a wall.

Danny lay and he lay and he thought and he thought, till he thought of a plan. Then he got up quickly and he ran and he ran, keeping close behind the wall so that the driver of the cart could not see him. He ran till he came to a place where the road turned a corner, and by now the cart was far behind him. Then he jumped over the wall and lay down in the middle of the road pretending to be dead.

He lay there a long time. He heard the cart coming nearer and nearer. He kept his eyes shut. He hoped the driver would see him and not run him over.

When the driver saw Danny lying stretched in the middle of the road, he stopped his cart and said, 'That's funny. That's the fox that was stealing my fish. That's the fox I hit with my whip. I thought I had only touched the tip of his tail, but now I see I must have hurt him badly. He must have run away from me ahead of my cart. And now he is dead.' He got down from his cart and stooped to look at Danny.

'What a beautiful red coat he's got,' the driver said, 'and what beautiful, thick red trousers. What a beautiful long bushy tail, with a beautiful white tip. What a beautiful long smooth nose with a beautiful black tip. I'll take him home with me, I think, and skin him and sell his fur.'

So he picked up Danny Fox and threw him on to the cart on top of the boxes of fish.

Key points

1. What was Danny's plan?
2. Why did the fisherman stop his cart?
3. Why was the fisherman surprised at what he saw?
4. What did the fisherman intend to do with Danny?
5. How had Danny's plan worked?

A closer look

Make a list of all the information you now have about the fox.

For talk

Talk about anything else you know about foxes and any stories
you have read about a fox.

For writing

Later in the story Danny said, 'I am always full of tricks.   I'm the
cleverest creature at tricks in all the world.'   Write a story about
Danny in which he tried to prove this was true.

Read on

Danny has many battles with the fisherman, but also helps him
when he has a problem.   Read about Danny's adventures in
Danny Fox by David Thomson.

7. It came in the night

Matthew likes new experiences but there is one he does not enjoy!

'Oh!' thought Matthew when he woke up next morning. 'Ow!'

Something had gone wrong with him in the night, and now he was hot and miserable all over, and his neck and his ears and his face were hurting.

It was another surprise, and a nasty one too.

'Ow!' he said again, and tried to see if he was lying on something hard, but it was much too sore for him to turn his head. He knew now that there must be something worse wrong with him than lying on a knobbly toy, but he didn't know what. It was horrid waking up like that when he had gone to bed quite well and ordinary.

'Mummy,' he cried, and he got out of bed and went stumbling into Daddy and Mummy's room.

'Whatever is it, Matthew?' said Mummy, grumpily because she didn't like being woken up.

'I'm all hot and sore and I hurt,' wailed Matthew, burrowing against her and really crying now.
'Something has hurt me in the night and I don't know what.'

'Pins and needles probably,' mumbled Daddy, lying quite still with his eyes shut. He never opened his eyes when Matthew came in in the morning, because he always hoped he could go back to sleep again.

'It doesn't sound like pins and needles,' said Mummy, and the bed-clothes heaved as she sat up and gathered Matthew on to her knee. 'Let's have a look,' she said, and then she saw Matthew's poor face. It was all fat and swollen tight at the sides, and his ears were sticking out like jug handles on top of the bulges. No wonder it felt sore.

'Oh no!' said Mummy. 'Poor old boy, you've got mumps, that's why you feel so horrid.'

Key points

1. What made Matthew certain there was something wrong with him?
2. What did he decide to do?
3. Why was his mother grumpy at first?
4. Why did his father keep his eyes shut?
5. What do you think made Matthew's mother sure he had mumps?

A closer look

Imagine Matthew's mother asked the doctor to come and have a look at Matthew.   Write down the information she gave the doctor about Matthew's symptoms.

For talk

Talk about your own memories of having mumps or measles or chicken-pox.

For writing

Children of Matthew's age learn a lot very quickly.   Think back to when you were younger and write about a new experience you can remember, which taught you a lesson.

Read on

Teresa Verschoyle's book *Matthew's Secret Surprises* describes many new experiences Matthew has.   When you read the book you can enjoy remembering how *you* felt on similar occasions.

8. What shall we do now?

Uncle Peder sells his wooden toys as he travels through the countryside. The one toy he will not sell is his favourite, a little wooden horse in which he keeps his money. But all is not well for Uncle Peder and his wooden horse.

Uncle Peder and the little wooden horse went on from village to village and found the same state of affairs. Nobody wanted Uncle Peder's toys now that they had new, cheap ones from the town. They didn't want his news either. No, thank you! They read all they wanted in the newspapers.

This was all very well, but Uncle Peder had to eat, and to pay for his food. One by one the coins disappeared as they came out of the neck of the little wooden horse. One day there were no more left at all.

'What shall we do, master?' said the little wooden horse.

'I must sell my toys cheaper,' said Uncle Peder. And he sold his beautiful wooden toys for fourpence, twopence, and even a penny, along the high road. Presently the sack was empty, and the little wooden horse had nothing left to carry at all.

'What shall we do now, master?' said the little wooden horse.

'Why, I'll sell my coat!' said Uncle Peder.

He sold his coat, and soon he was shivering, while his shoes let in the wet.

'What use are shoes with holes in them?' said Uncle Peder. So he sold those too; but the money soon went.

Now they were in a bad way. No toys, no money, no coat, no shoes, no paint on the little wooden horse, no food, and Uncle Peder shivering and aching all over!

'Master is ill,' said the little wooden horse. 'I'll go and sell myself.'

So when they had settled themselves in a barn for the night, and Uncle Peder had fallen into an uneasy sleep, the little wooden horse trundled out into the moonlight and away on his little wooden wheels as fast as he could go.

Key points

1. Why did the villagers no longer want Uncle Peder's toys and news?
2. What did Uncle Peder decide to do with the toys, to earn some money?
3. What else did he do to try to earn some money?
4. Why did Uncle Peder become ill?
5. Why did the wooden horse decide to leave Uncle Peder?

A closer look

Everything seemed to have gone wrong for Uncle Peder. Make a list of all the unfortunate things that had happened to him.

For talk

Uncle Peder made beautiful toys. Talk about any toys that you have had that seemed to you to be beautiful.

For writing

When Uncle Peder woke up the little wooden horse was a long way away. Write two more paragraphs for the story.   The first should tell what Uncle Peder thought when he woke up.   The second should tell what had happened to the little wooden horse by then.

Read on

The little wooden horse's adventures take him across the sea, down a coal-mine and even into a treasure cave. All the time he is trying to earn money to help Uncle Peder.   Read what happens to them both in *Adventures of the Little Wooden Horse* by Ursula Moray Williams.

9. A plot in the forest

The small animals of the forest have a lot of fun, but they must always be on the watch for the owl and the fox.

It happened that a long time ago Terrible Owl had made up his mind to catch Pleasant Fieldmouse and plunge him in a stew, but the fieldmouse was always too sly and too fast and seldom ventured out at night. In the strong daylight Terrible Owl was half blind and had to swim through a sunny fog.

However, Tired Fox, whose feet generally ached from long, difficult chases (difficult since the forest was full of popholes – those are holes to pop into – and full of secret chinks and slippery caves just right for escapers to hide in), had come across a recipe for Hedgehog Pie. Actually it was Chipmunk Pie, but he was willing to substitute ingredients.

Mrs Worry-Wind Hedgehog, the world's best worrier, was so constantly afraid of getting caught that she would dance out of her house like a spinning top, watching out in all directions.

So it was that the two would-be cooks got together. 'You help me, I'll help you,' suggested the clever fox. They shook a paw and a wing, and the moon hid behind a cloud.

Soon after, Tired Fox let it be known he was going on a trip. 'I'm going on a trip! I'm going on a trip!' he would casually sing, skipping up and down the path, waving a flag. When the great day arrived, he left by canoe, and everybody saw him merrily off. Up the stream he floated, singing still. The forest folk gorgeously celebrated.

Key points

1. Why was daylight like a *sunny fog* to Terrible Owl?
2. Why do you think the fox was called *Tired* Fox?
3. Why do you think the moon hid behind a cloud, when the fox and the owl shook a paw and a wing?
4. Why do you think the forest folk celebrated when Tired Fox left for his trip?
5. Tired Fox had a plan.   What do you think it was?

A closer look

Explain why Terrible Owl wanted to catch Pleasant Fieldmouse
and why he had never succeeded.   Then explain why Tired Fox wanted
to catch Mrs Worry-Wind Hedgehog and why *he* had never succeeded.

For talk

Hedgehog Pie may sound nice to a fox!   Talk about the pies *you*
like and why they are your favourites.

For writing

Tired Fox was full of tricks (just like Danny Fox in an earlier
story.)   Write about any tricks you have played on other people
and what happened when you played them.

Read on

Does Tired Fox really go on a trip?   Read what happens, and more of the
funny stories of the forest folk, in *Pleasant Fieldmouse* by Jan Wahl.

10. Inside the doll's house

Elizabeth has always wondered what happens inside her dolls' house when she is not there. She also has a toy monkey which seems able to talk and is always playing tricks. It is the monkey that tells her how to get into the dolls' house.

At this moment Elizabeth heard a patter of steps and a flurried voice inside.

She put her ear down and listened.

'Here she is! What did I tell you!' said the voice. 'Now, are we all ready to begin? She's very prompt!'

And the door was opened by a lady with very red cheeks (very red indeed; too red, thought Elizabeth), and a frizzy fringe of dark hair, over which was a rather battered hat with a bluish feather. The feather drooped sadly, as if it had been dipped in some soup. She looked at Elizabeth severely, under her fringe.

'Come in,' she said. 'We were quite expecting you. In fact, you're a little late.'

'Well!' said Elizabeth, 'I heard you say quite plainly I was very prompt!'

'You shouldn't listen through letter-boxes,' said the red-cheeked lady, and her feather bobbed angrily. 'If you're that sort of a maid, I'll send you straight away again.'

'Oh, but I'm not a maid at all –' began Elizabeth.

'No, no, I know you're not. You're a char, sent to help with the spring-cleaning. I ordered you myself, so I should know. Come in, do.'

And without thinking twice about it, Elizabeth walked into the house. She said nothing (she was too surprised) but followed the red-cheeked person into the parlour.

Here a most strange sight met her eyes. There was a

young lady flopped all over a chair (which was really too small for her, anyway) and with a very lackadaisical look. But the strangest thing of all was ... that she had only a vest and a hat on.   It was a blue knitted vest, with a great many dropped stitches.

'Oh, I say –' began Elizabeth.

'That's all right.   Never mind Lupin,' said the red-cheeked lady in a loud whisper behind her hand.   'She's always a little queer the way she dresses, you know. She's not quite right in the top, you see.'

'But she *is*!' said Elizabeth.   'She's perfectly all right! I'll never leave a doll half-dressed again.   It's dreadful for her!   Where are her clothes?   I'll put them on.'

'You'll do no such thing,' said Vanessa (for Elizabeth had realized that it was her doll Vanessa, and was not at all surprised to see that she was head of the house.   She was an old-fashioned doll who had belonged to Elizabeth's grandmother, and had always been a managing person, it was those red cheeks).   'You'll do no such thing!   Why, I employed you as a char, not as a lady's maid.   You'd better begin.'

Key points

1. What could Elizabeth hear through the door of her dolls' house?
2. How did Elizabeth get inside the dolls' house?
3. Why do you think the doll called Lupin was so badly dressed?
4. Why was Elizabeth not surprised that Vanessa was in charge in the dolls' house?
5. Why do you think the dolls did not seem to recognise Elizabeth?

A closer look

All the questions are about Elizabeth's doll, Vanessa. Answer them without looking back at the passage. Then look back to check your answers, and answer any questions you could not do.

1. Who was Vanessa?
2. Who had first owned Vanessa?
3. What position did Vanessa seem to have inside the dolls' house?
4. What was noticeable about her cheeks?
5. What was noticeable about her hair?
6. What sort of hat did Vanessa wear?
7. Who did Vanessa think Elizabeth was?
8. Why had she been expecting Elizabeth?
9. Why was she annoyed with Elizabeth?
10. Where did Vanessa take Elizabeth?
11. What did Vanessa think about Lupin, the doll in the blue vest?
12. Why did she stop Elizabeth dressing Lupin properly?
13. What did Vanessa mean when she said to Elizabeth, 'You'd better begin.'?
14. How did Vanessa show she was a *managing* person?
15. What else can you say about the way Vanessa behaved?

For talk

Most children pretend their toy animals and dolls can come to life and even talk. Talk about any that you have had that you brought to life.

FOUR AND EIGHT

The Foxglove by the cottage door
Looks down on Joe, and Joe is four.

The Foxglove by the garden gate
Looks down on Joan, and Joan is eight.

'I'm glad we're small,' said Joan. 'I love
To see inside the fox's glove,
Where taller people cannot see,
And all is ready for the bee;
The door is wide, the feast is spread,
The walls are dotted rosy red.'
'And only little people know
How nice it looks in there,' said Joe.
Said Joan, 'The upper rooms are locked;
A bee went buzzing up – he knocked,
But no one let him in, so then
He bumbled gaily down again.'
'Oh dear!' sighed Joe, 'if only we
Could grow as little as that bee,
We too might room by room explore
The Foxglove by the cottage door.'

The Foxglove by the garden gate
Looked down and smiled on Four and Eight.

Ffrida Wolfe

For writing

As Joe said in the poem it would be nice to grow small enough to explore
inside a foxglove.   Somehow Elizabeth *was* able to get inside her dolls' house.
Write a story in which you suddenly shrank to a size where you could
get into something much smaller than yourself.

Read on

Now that Elizabeth is able to get into the dolls' house, she finds
out a lot about how the dolls live.   She also finds out how she
could improve the dolls' lives when she is back to her normal
size.   All the time she has to watch out for the mischievous
monkey.   Read the amusing, half-real, half make-believe, stories
of Elizabeth and her dolls in *Five Dolls in a House* by Helen Clare.

11. The horse that wanted a boy

Up to now, Mike has led a normal life with his mother and father, and sister Gloria.   One day, on his way home from school, something very strange happens.

Mike got off the school bus with a lot of other children, but he didn't walk home with any of them because he wanted to see if he could find some good rocks for his rock collection.

So nobody was with him when he saw the horse.

The horse was just standing there, and Mike was surprised because he had never seen a horse anywhere near his house before.

Mike got up out of the ditch, where he'd been looking for rocks, and went over to the horse.

'Hello, horsie.   Where did you come from?' he asked.

'Well,' the horse said, 'I was just here, waiting for the school bus.'

'Hey!   Was that you talking?' Mike asked.

'Of course,' the horse said.   'You don't see any other horse around, do you?'

'Well, no,' Mike said.

The horse bent over to eat some grass.   Finally Mike said, 'I didn't know horses could talk, though.'

'Have you ever talked to a horse?'

'No,' Mike said.

'Well, then,' the horse said.

Mike wondered what he meant by that remark, but he waited a while and then he said, 'Why were you waiting for the school bus?'

'I was hoping some boy would take me home to live with him.   You see, I don't have a boy.'

'I wish you could live with me, but we don't have a barn, or anything like that.   Nobody around here does.'

'A garage will be all right.'

'Really?   You mean you'll come home with me, and be my own horse?'

'No.   *You'll* be *my* boy.'

Key points

1.   What was Mike doing when he noticed the horse?
2.   Why was he surprised to see the horse?
3.   Why was the horse waiting for the school bus?
4.   How did the horse respond to Mike's surprise that it could talk?
5.   Why was the last line of the passage another surprise?

A closer look

Write down all the information you now have about the horse.
Start with what seemed the most normal thing about it and end
with what seemed the most strange.

For talk

Talk about what you would need to do and to know, if you had a horse.
Compare looking after a horse with looking after any other pets you have.

For writing

Imagine *you* met an animal that wanted to come home with you
and make *you* its pet!   Make up the conversation you had with it.

Read on

Mike calls the horse Casey.   Casey is *very* unusual.   Not only
can he talk but he also has some strange ideas.   He thinks Mike
is *his* boy, he wants clothes to wear and to go to parties.   You
will enjoy *Casey the Utterly Impossible Horse* by Anita Feagles.

29

12. An alphabetical family

A family of mice live in the organ loft of a church.
One day they find a large balloon with a bag attached to it.
In the bag is a poor little mouse, who has escaped from the
Home for Waif-mice and Stray-mice.

'You can come and live with us,' said Mrs Peck. 'One more mouth to feed won't be a disaster. That is,' she added, 'if you'd like to be a Cupboardosity.'

'A Cupboardosity?' echoed the mouse doubtfully.

'That's a mouse who lives in a cupboard,' explained Uncle Washington.

'An organ loft cupboard,' added Uncle Ponty. 'Don't forget that. Most important.'

'Sometimes you'd help in the shop,' said Mr Peck.

'And sometimes in the house,' added his wife.

'We all take it in turns,' said Uncle Ponty.

'Most of us,' interrupted Uncle Washington meaningly. 'Some of us take more turns than others.'

'In the summer we go fruit-picking,' said Mr Peck hastily. 'Storing up things for the winter.'

'Strawberries,' said Uncle Ponty, drooling at the thought. 'And in the autumn it's nuts and black-berries.'

The mouse thought for a moment, still hardly able to believe the sudden change in his fortunes. 'It sounds very nice –' he began.

'T,' broke in Mrs Peck. 'If he stays he'll have to have a name and it must begin with "T".'

'Ma always likes to have her children named alphabetically,' explained Mr Peck. 'It's much less trouble in the long run.'

'I'm Aristotle,' said the tallest of the Pecks' off-spring, holding out his paw. 'I helped carry you up the stairs.' He pointed to the row of eager

faces behind him. 'This is Blaze and this is Cadwallader. Behind him there's Desdemona, Ethel, Francesca, Gaston, Hildegard, Iolanthe, Justin and Kean.'

'And I'm Ludowick,' the next mouse in the line stepped forward as Aristotle paused for breath. 'And this is Mordecat, Napoleon, Osborn, Peregrine, Quentin, Rowena and Sylvester.'

Key points

1. What did Mrs Peck mean when she said, 'One more mouth to feed won't be a disaster'?
2. What was a Cupboardosity?
3. Why do you think the new mouse could hardly believe what was happening?
4. Why did his name have to begin with T?
5. What did Mr Peck mean when he said, 'It's much less trouble in the long run'?

A closer look

Write down all that you now know about the Cupboardosity family and their life.

For talk

Mr and Mrs Peck's children were all given names in the order of the alphabet. See how many letters of the alphabet you can use, that begin the names of children in your school.

For writing

The Cupboardosities did different things in different seasons. Write four paragraphs, one for each season, in which you say what *you* like to do best of all in that season.

Read on

The new mouse is given the name Thursday, as that is the day he arrives and, of course, it begins with T. Thursday soon settles down and is full of good intentions but sometimes things go wrong! Read about his entertaining life in *Here Comes Thursday!* by Michael Bond.

13. Watch out for dinosaurs!

Jed is looking after two dinosaurs that have been found in his village. They have been hibernating for millions of years. One is called Dino and the other Sauro. Each morning the dinosaurs go down to the river to bathe.

Jed ran through the village, over the bridge and down on to the river bank, laughing out loud when he saw four ears sticking up out of the water like submarine periscopes. Several ducks, tails flapping, were keeping well out of the way.

'Out you come, Dino, and you too, Sauro,' he ordered. He whistled and waited. He was used to waiting. Eventually, Dino's neck rose up slowly like a conning tower and Sauro's followed. Their tails floated on the top of the water as they walked towards the bank. Dino lowered his head for Jed to tickle behind his ears. One day Sauro will do the same thing, thought Jed, looking fondly at the two great beasts lumbering out of the water.

The village was already stirring as Jed led the animals back through the street. Any day now the judges would be coming for the second time to inspect the village for the Best-Kept Village competition. There had been great activity during the past few weeks. Gardens and grass verges had been tidied and window boxes replanted. Some shop-fronts had been repainted, the war memorial had been scoured and all the inn signs had been cleaned.

The Parish Clerk, like a general in command, stood on his front doorstep, looking sharply up and down the street for the least trace of litter or untidiness. Jed wished Dino and Sauro would hurry. Their large bodies nearly filled the street and their heads reached over the rooftops. They ambled along at snail's pace.

When the Parish Clerk saw them, he ran forward waving his arms and shouting, 'Get those beasts back to the recreation ground, Jed.'

Key points

1. Why did the dinosaurs' ears make Jed laugh?
2. How do you know Dino was tamer than Sauro?
3. How had the village prepared for the competition?
4. Why did the Parish Clerk seem like a general?
5. Why do you think he wanted Jed to take the dinosaurs back to the recreation ground?

A closer look

Imagine you were near the bridge, watching Jed and the dinosaurs.   Write down what you saw.

For talk

Most people are interested in dinosaurs.   Talk about what you know about them and why you think they are so interesting.

For writing

Write a story about the day the judges came to inspect the village and what Dino and Sauro did that day.

Read on

Large dinosaurs and Best-Kept Villages do not go well together! Read about all the unlikely happenings in *Two Village Dinosaurs* by Phyllis Arkle.

14. A very odd ball

Sarah and Rufus are playing in their garden. Sarah hears a buzzing noise coming from under a bush. To their surprise they find an object like a ball, which seems to be able to move on its own.

The ball had begun to buzz much more loudly and, as Rufus pointed excitedly, a small window opened on its underside. Slowly, something that looked like a tiny crane unfolded itself from the window. It moved outwards and downwards. On the end of the crane arm there was a small scoop.

The children saw a furry caterpillar looping its way through the grass. Then, all of a sudden, the scoop snatched up the caterpillar and, before you could say 'Jack', let alone 'Robinson', the crane and its wildly wriggling prisoner had disappeared into the ball. The window clicked shut.

'Do you think it eats caterpillars?' Sarah asked in amazement.

'I don't know. Let's try to find it another one.'

While the children searched, the ginger cat, who lived in the next-door cottage, made himself thin enough to squeeze through his favourite gap in the hedge and he padded towards the ball. He studied it for a moment and then, bending low, curled out one paw to give it a playful tap.

The ball gave a loud HOOT and rolled quickly into the nearest flowerbed.

'I think,' said Sarah, 'that ball's afraid of Tizer.'

Rufus was carefully parting the leaves to look at the ball again. Sarah hung back a little.

'Perhaps it doesn't like being stared at.'

'Why ever not?'

'It's rude.'

'Don't be daft.　It's only staring at people that's rude. How can a ball possibly mind?'

It was then that the most extraordinary thing of all happened.

The ball spoke!

Key points

1.　What came out of the ball?
2.　How was the caterpillar captured?
3.　What effect did Tizer, the cat, have on the ball?
4.　What did Rufus do next?
5.　Why was Sarah cautious about the ball?

A closer look

Imagine Sarah was asked later to describe the ball to her class.
Write down what she said, using only the information in the passage.

For talk

You may not find anything so strange as a ball that can talk!　Talk about any objects you *have* found that seemed to you to be very interesting or unusual.

For writing

Write two more paragraphs for the story.
The first one should be the one *before* the passage starts.
The second one should be the one *after* the passage ends.

Read on

Can the ball speak, or is there something else inside the ball?
Find out the answer and what happens to Sarah, Rufus and the ball, in *Zozu the Robot* by Diana Carter.

15. Nobody takes any notice

The Wombles are worried because the Human Beings make so much litter and pollution. Bungo, the youngest Womble, is determined to make a Human Being listen to him about the problem.

Bright and early the next morning Bungo, fairly bursting with self-importance, set out across the Common with his tidy-bag. He picked up a bus ticket here and a lemonade tin there and a copy of *The Times* (yesterday's) for Great Uncle Bulgaria and all the time he was chattering away to himself, saying:

'I bet, I jolly well bet, I get a Human Being person to listen to ME!'

Which, as even his Womble friends didn't bother to listen to Bungo half the time, was a bit unlikely. And even he wasn't quite silly enough to venture off the Common, so he watched from a safe distance as the Japanese gentleman drove off to work in his enormous car, followed by Mr Frogmorton who, as usual, was dropping litter behind him in his absent-minded way.

'Tck, tck, tck,' said Bungo, sounding just like Tobermory, and then his little heart began to go 'thump thump thump' because coming towards him across the grass was a postman riding a bicycle.

'Now or never,' mumbled Bungo and he stepped out from behind the bushes and said politely:

''Morning.'

The postman took no notice at all. He just went on his way whistling to himself.

Bungo stared after him, shook his head and tidied up a couple of paper-bags. And then,

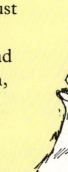

even louder than the thumping noise his heart had
made, he heard a steady clump clump clump, and a very
smart lady riding a beautiful horse came round the corner.
Now Wombles are just a little bit nervous of horses, so
it was really extremely brave of Bungo to step forward
and say very politely:

'Good morning, Madam.'

But the lady only trotted past with her head in the air,
although the horse did give Bungo a look out of the
corner of its eyes which made that young Womble step
smartly back into the bushes again.

'It's very odd,' said Bungo, 'but Human Beings just
don't seem to want to take any notice. Hallo, here comes
someone else. Oh dear, it's a Someone and a dog.'

Bungo was rather nervous about dogs. In fact he had
once climbed right to the top of a very tall tree to avoid one.

'N-n-now or n-n-never,' muttered Bungo and with his
fur going all spiky with worry he climbed out of the bush
and in a deep, husky voice quite unlike his own, he said:

'How do you do?'

The Human Being appeared to be thinking deeply
about other things, for he took no notice of Bungo and
just walked on across the Common.

'Hallo – dog?' said Bungo desperately.

But the dog, as deep in thought as its master, didn't
even bother to bark.

Key points

1. Why was Bungo carrying a tidy-bag?
2. What else did he intend to do that day?
3. Why do you think he watched the Japanese gentleman and Mr Frogmorton *from a safe distance*?
4. What did the three Human Beings do when Bungo spoke to them on the Common?
5. What did the two animals do?

A closer look

A. The passage can be divided into five parts:-

Part 1   is about Bungo on the Common, picking up litter.
Part 2   is about Bungo watching people go to work.
Part 3   is about Bungo meeting the postman.
Part 4   is about Bungo meeting the lady on the horse.
Part 5   is about Bungo meeting the man and his dog.

Do the following for each of the five parts:-

1. Give each part a title.
2. Write down what Bungo was doing.
3. Write down what he could see, *or* what happened to him.
4. Write down what you think *he* was thinking.

B. Imagine the only information you had about the Wombles was in the passage.   Write down what you now know about them.

For talk

The Wombles could not make the Human Beings listen to them. Talk about any times when someone hasn't listened to you or you haven't listened to someone else.

NEIGHBOURS

The people who live on the right of us
Are very quiet and make no fuss,
But the family on the left clatter about
Day and night, and sometimes shout.

Yet the people on the left of us
Are really rather marvellous;
Instead of being put out by everything
They burst out laughing and sing.
But the family who live on the right of us
Often make me curious,
The way the father whispers to the mother,
The sister to her silent brother.

I suppose that neighbours are meant
To be different.

Leonard Clark

For writing

The neighbours on the right in the poem seem like the people Bungo met on the Common. None of them says very much. The neighbours on the left are noisy but more interesting. Write about any interesting people you know, the sort of people who will tell you interesting things and listen to what you have to say.

Read on

Will anyone listen to Bungo? Can he and the other Wombles make the Human Beings take more care? Find out in *Wombling Free* by Elisabeth Beresford.

16. A shock for the teacher

The girl who tells this story is eight years old. She has a magic finger which tingles when someone really annoys her. When the Magic Finger is upon someone, things begin to happen!

Poor old Mrs Winter.

One day we were in class, and she was teaching us spelling. 'Stand up,' she said to me, 'and spell *cat*.'

'That's an easy one,' I said. '*K-a-t*.'

'You are a stupid little girl!' Mrs Winter said.

'I am not a stupid little girl!' I cried. 'I am a very nice little girl!'

'Go and stand in the corner,' Mrs Winter said.

Then I got cross, and I saw red, and I put the Magic Finger on Mrs Winter good and strong, and almost at once . . .

Guess what?

Whiskers began growing out of her face! They were long black whiskers, just like the ones you see on a cat, only much bigger. And how fast they grew! Before we had time to think, they were out to her ears!

Of course the whole class started screaming with laughter, and then Mrs Winter said, 'Will you be so kind as to tell me what you find so madly funny, all of you?'

And when she turned around to write something on the blackboard we saw that she had grown a *tail* as well! It was a huge bushy tail!

I cannot begin to tell you what happened after that, but if any of you are wondering whether Mrs Winter is quite all right again now the answer is No. And she never will be.

Key points

1. Why was Mrs Winter angry?
2. What made the girl use the Magic Finger on Mrs Winter?
3. What made the class scream with laughter?
4. What are we *not* told in the last paragraph?
5. How much do you think Mrs Winter deserved her punishment?

A closer look

Imagine *you* were Mrs Winter.   Tell the story of what happened to you in the classroom.

For talk

Talk about magic and whether you believe in it or not.

For writing

Funny things happen in classrooms, even if they are not quite like what happened to Mrs Winter.   Write about any funny incidents you remember in *your* classroom.

Read on

The main victims of the Magic Finger are the Gregg family.
They spend a lot of time hunting.
The owner of the Magic Finger does not like hunters!
Read what happens to them in *The Magic Finger* by Roald Dahl.

17. A scarecrow's life

*Susan and John are on holiday on the farm where their old friend,
the scarecrow Worzel Gummidge, lives.   The children have dressed
up as scarecrows for a fancy dress competition.   They have
come to show Worzel Gummidge what they look like.*

Worzel Gummidge was sitting on the little ladder that
led up to the door of the old caravan.   As soon as he saw
Susan and John he got up and began to wave his arms.

'Go away!' he shouted.   'We don't want no more scarecrows.'

'It's only us,' said John.

'It's a great deal too bad.   Ooh aye! it's a great deal
more than a great deal too bad.   Turning yourselves into
scarecrows and trying to take the food out of other
scarecrows' mouths.'

Susan glanced at Gummidge's muddy mouth and gave
a little shudder.

'We wouldn't do that, really we wouldn't,' she said.
'We wouldn't *like* to.'

Gummidge looked at her in a disbelieving sort of way,
and Susan, thinking that he might be pleased to see the
hedgehog, rolled it out of her apron.

'Go and find your own hairbrushes,' said Gummidge
angrily, 'and don't go using mine.'

'We were only bringing it back to you,' said Susan.

'A likely story when it's got legs of its own.'
Gummidge jerked himself on to the grass and the
hedgehog scurried up to him and began to rub its bristles
against the straw of Gummidge's boots.

'It does shoe-cleaning and all sorts,' he remarked
proudly.   'Worth its weight in turnips that hairbrush is.'

As Gummidge seemed to be in a slightly better
temper, John and Susan told him about the fête at
Penfold and why they had dressed up as scarecrows.

'We shan't go on being scarecrows after to-day,' she added.

'You'll not be able to stop yourselves,' said Gummidge gloomily, 'no more than chickens can stop being chickens once they've started.   They never turns back into eggs again.'

Key points

1.   Why were Susan and John dressed up as scarecrows?
2.   Why was Worzel Gummidge annoyed when he saw the children?
3.   Why did Susan shudder when she looked at Gummidge?
4.   What did Gummidge use the hedgehog for?
5.   What did Gummidge expect would happen to the children?

A closer look

Gummidge's moods changed a lot.   Write down what sort of mood he was in:

1.   when he told the children to go away;
2.   when Susan said they did not want his food;
3.   when Susan showed him the hedgehog;
4.   when the hedgehog began to brush his boots;
5.   when he was talking about chickens and eggs.

For talk

Imagine you were going to the fête in fancy dress.   Talk about what you would dress up as.

For writing

Later in the story Susan and John pretended to be real scarecrows. Imagine you did the same and write a story called 'A Scarecrow for an Hour'.

Read on

Everyone enjoys the funny books about Worzel Gummidge.   The grumbly scarecrow is always causing problems for his human friends.   The passage you have read is from one of the books, *Worzel Gummidge Again* by Barbara Euphan Todd.

18. The game of his life

Brinsly is a goalkeeper. He is so keen on football that sometimes he even plays in his dreams!

Brinsly was pushed on to the field. A band was already playing. Then Brinsly saw them, his sister Patricia and her school friends, and lots of girls from Plum Lane Junior School. They were pretending to be majorettes. They were dressed in majorette costume and were waving batons. Patricia was in the lead and waving a huge baton. The crowd cheered. The band followed the majorettes.

Then, to Brinsly's horror, he saw his mother. His mother was banging a huge drum. The drum was sitting on Mother's chest and looked much too heavy for her. But Mother smiled and banged away.

Brinsly made as if to run up to Mother but the whistle blew for the kick-off. The game began.

Brinsly was in goal as usual. But he never had to work so hard. Balls seemed to come at him from all directions. He jumped, headed, dived from side to side. The crowd roared. They chanted:

'Come on, goalie,' *clap, clap*.

'Come on, goalie,' *clap, clap*.

'Come on, goalie,' *clap clap*.

Brinsly felt tired, yet he kept on. Balls from the right were saved, balls from the left were saved too and the high balls were headed. In the end, Brinsly felt so tired he just could not go on any more. He badly wanted to sit down or simply lie down and go to sleep. He felt his eyes closing. The cheers from the fans got further and further away. He felt himself slipping to the ground. He told himself that he must keep on. He could not though. He just fell down.

Key points

1. Why was Brinsly's sister, Patricia, at the match?
2. Why do you think Brinsly was surprised when he saw his mother?
3. How did the crowd help Brinsly?
4. Why did Brinsly begin to feel so tired?
5. What do you think happened to him at the end?

A closer look

Brinsly *was* dreaming.   Imagine that next morning he told his sister about his dream.   Write down what he said.

For talk

Talk about what you like (and dislike) about football and any other games played with a ball.

For writing

Brinsly liked to dream he was a star goalkeeper. Imagine you were dreaming about a day when you became a star at something. Write the story of your dream day.

Read on

Is Brinsly dreaming or is he really playing?   You can find out about Brinsly and his team in *Brinsly's Dream* by Petronella Breinburg.

19. Abandoned kitten

*A kitten has been abandoned by its owners, when they
moved away.   No one seems to want to give it a home.
As the weather grows cold, it finds shelter in a garden shed.*

The kitten hadn't gone far this time, only as far as the
ground in front of the cottages where it sat waiting
hopefully for someone to appear with food.   Eventually
it was Mr Reece who, while his wife was busy washing
up, brought out a basinful of meat scraps and bread
soaked in gravy.   He made a great show of putting down
the basin where he could be certain Miss Coker would
see him doing it.   But he did not wait to see the food
consumed.   He had been sternly ordered not to stay out
in the cold.

The kitten had eaten no more than a mouthful before
it was set upon by the gulls, who had now been joined
by a company of rooks and jackdaws.   Buffeted on all
sides, twice knocked off its feet and terrified by the
savage pecks aimed at its eyes, the kitten ran off to its
old retreat under the wall.   Here it crouched and
watched while the squawking quarrelling gang emptied
the basin and flew off.

After wandering aimlessly about for the rest of the day
it went back to the shed.   Having been homeless for a
fortnight it was content to have found at least
a dry sleeping place.

The Reece children had seen the rooks and gulls
attacking the kitten and would have run out to chase
them away, but by the time they had changed their shoes
and put on their coats and mufflers the birds had gone,
leaving nothing but an empty basin.

Key points

1. What was the kitten waiting for?
2. Why did the birds attack the kitten?
3. Why was Mr Reece unable to help the kitten, when it was attacked?
4. Why were the Reece children unable to help it?
5. What was the one thing that made the kitten's life easier?

A closer look

Make a list of the people in the passage. Write down what each of them seemed to feel about the kitten, and what they did about it.

For talk

The wild birds stole the kitten's food. They were hungry too, in the cold weather. Talk about the birds that come to be fed in the winter and what people can give them to eat.

For writing

The kitten was finding life very hard. Imagine there was a hard frost and snow during the night. Write a story about the kitten's next morning.

Read on

What will happen to the kitten, lonely, cold and hungry? The owner of the shed seems to have no feelings for it. Nobody else seems able to help. Read what happens in *The Snow Kitten* by Nina Warner Hooke.

20. An unexpected find

Sandy's mother works in a builder's office.   Sandy and his friend, Mike, have been doing some shopping for her after school.   On their way back to the office, they take a short cut through the builder's yard.

The yard gate was wide open.   Sandy knew what that meant.   The big van wasn't back for the night.   The small one wasn't parked in its usual place either.

'Some of them must still be out working,' said Sandy. 'We'll have to hurry before they come in.'

But Mike didn't want to hurry.   He stood staring at the washbasins, lengths of pipe, stacks of wood and long ladders.

'I'd like to be a builder,' said Mike, and before Sandy could stop him he had nipped into the shed where the special wood and the big saws were kept.

'Come out,' hissed Sandy, standing in the doorway and peering into the darkness inside.   'If Mr Bell finds us we'll get into awful trouble.'

The shed was suddenly lit up and Mike shot out.

'Headlights,' said Sandy.   'It's the big van coming in.'

Sandy ran to the back door and Mike followed him into the office.   Sandy's mother had locked up and was waiting for them.

They all went back to the flat together and had tea. After that it was television and games until Mike's father came to collect him.   The boys went into Sandy's bedroom to fetch Mike's things.

'What's that stuff all over my bed?' said Sandy, as Mike picked up his coat.

'Where?' said Mike.   'Oh, it's come out of my pocket.'

'It's sawdust!' said Sandy.   'Did you take it from the woodshed in the yard?'

Mike nodded.   'From that big bin in the corner.   It's

for my guinea pig's cage.   I only took a few handfuls.
Here, can you find something to put it in?'

Sandy ran out to the kitchen and came back with a
paper bag.   Mike had gathered the sawdust into a pile.

'Your Dad says hurry up,' said Sandy.   He helped
Mike scoop the sawdust into the bag.   'Look, here's
some money.'

'Well, it's not mine,' said Mike.   'I emptied that
pocket right out before I put the sawdust in.'

Sandy blew at the coin which lay in his hand.

'Come along, Mike,' his father called, and they heard
the front door of the flat open.

'See you,' said Mike and ran.

Sandy stayed there, staring at the coin in his hand.   It
was a small silver coin, old and worn, but he could just
make out on one side the head of a woman and the word
ANNA.   It didn't belong to Mike.   And it quite certainly
hadn't been on his bedspread before Mike put his things
there.   It must have come with the sawdust, thought
Sandy.   But if it had, then what was a strange silver coin
doing in the sawdust bin in the builder's yard?

Key points

1. Why were Mike and Sandy in the builder's yard?
2. Why was Sandy worried when Mike went into the shed?
3. What made them hurry out of the yard?
4. What did Mike take from the builder's yard?
5. Why was Sandy sure the silver coin came from the yard?

A closer look

A. Each of the following is from the *first* part of the passage you
    have read.   They are in the wrong order.   Try to put them in
    the right order.

    1. Sandy ran to the back door.
    2. They all went back to the flat together.
    3. Mike didn't want to hurry.
    4. The yard gate was wide open.
    5. Mike nipped into the shed.
    6. Sandy's mother was waiting for them.
    7. 'We'll have to hurry before they come in.'
    8. The shed was suddenly lit up.

B. Now do the same with these, which are from the *second* part
    of the passage.   When you have finished, check to see if you
    had all sixteen in the right order.

    1. 'What's that stuff all over my bed?'
    2. What was a strange silver coin doing in the sawdust bin?
    3. 'See you,' said Mike and ran.
    4. Sandy blew at the coin which lay in his hand.
    5. 'Look, here's some money.'
    6. Mike's father came to collect him.
    7. Mike had gathered the sawdust into a pile.
    8. Sandy stayed there, staring at the coin in his hand.

For talk

Mike said he would like to be a builder, and he went into the
shed to look round.   Do you think he should have done?

THE BLACK PEBBLE

There went three children down to the shore,
Down to the shore and back;
There was skipping Susan and bright-eyed Sam
And little scowling Jack.

Susan found a white cockle-shell,
The prettiest ever seen,
And Sam picked up a piece of glass
Rounded and smooth and green.

But Jack found only a plain black pebble
That lay by the rolling sea,
And that was all that ever he found;
So back they all went three.

The cockle-shell they put on the table,
The green glass on the shelf,
But the little black pebble that Jack had found,
He kept it for himself.

James Reeves

For writing

Jack's black pebble and Sandy's silver coin were both valuable,
but in different ways.   Write about the things you think are *your*
treasures, how you got them and why you like them so much.

Read on

A silver coin is a strange thing to find in a sawdust bin.   Could it
be one of the antiques that are missing from the houses nearby?
Read how Sandy tries to find out in *The Sawdust Secret* by Jean Wills.

21. Grandma's new dog

Billy's grandma has been out shopping and has brought a dog home with her!

The dog that grandma had brought back was not exactly a beauty. Steven – who was married to Billy's sister – said it would win first prize in any Ugly Competition. And he wasn't far off the mark. Even grandma called it a liquorice allsort to its face. That was because it appeared to have so many different sorts of breed in it.

Neither was it what you might call sensible. It was as daft as a brush, dashing about from pillar to post, knocking things over, and jumping up on your lap. Steven kept saying it had ants in its pants.

Grandma had got it from the R.S.P.C.A. man in the market. He had told her that lots of people were buying dogs for pets and then losing interest in them in no time. They turned them loose in the streets.

'It's a crying shame!' grandma had said. 'What happens to them after that?'

'If they're lucky, somebody brings them to us, madam. Then they're our problem. We'd like to keep them forever, of course. But I'm afraid we can't. Our finances won't allow it. We keep them a fortnight, then we have to get rid of them – one way or another.'

That was how grandma came to get the dog. The R.S.P.C.A. man had given her a bit of string to lead it away with and a free booklet called *Keeping Your Dog Happy* which consisted mostly of advertisements for worming tablets.

'Well I couldn't just leave it behind, Our Alice,' said grandma. 'Could I?'

Billy's mam said nothing.

'That dog'll be a nuisance,' said Billy's dad. 'Just mark my words.'

'It's as good as gold,' said grandma.

Key points

1. Why was the dog in the care of the R.S.P.C.A.?
2. Why had Billy's grandma brought the dog home?
3. What help had the R.S.P.C.A. man given her?
4. Why did she call the dog a liquorice allsort?
5. What do you think Billy's mother felt about the dog?

A closer look

Use the passage to make two lists. The first should give the reasons for keeping the dog, the second for *not* keeping it.

For talk

Billy's grandma had decided to take the dog *on the spur of the moment.* Talk about any times when you have done something on the spur of the moment.

For writing

Billy's dad said the dog would be a nuisance. His grandma said the dog was as good as gold. Write a story about the dog's first day in the house, when it proved *both* were right.

Read on

Billy's dad is quite right. The dog soon begins to cause problems. There are more serious problems when Billy's dad loses his job. Read what happens to the family, and the dog, in *Old Dog, New Tricks* by Dick Cate.

22. A crocodile comes to stay

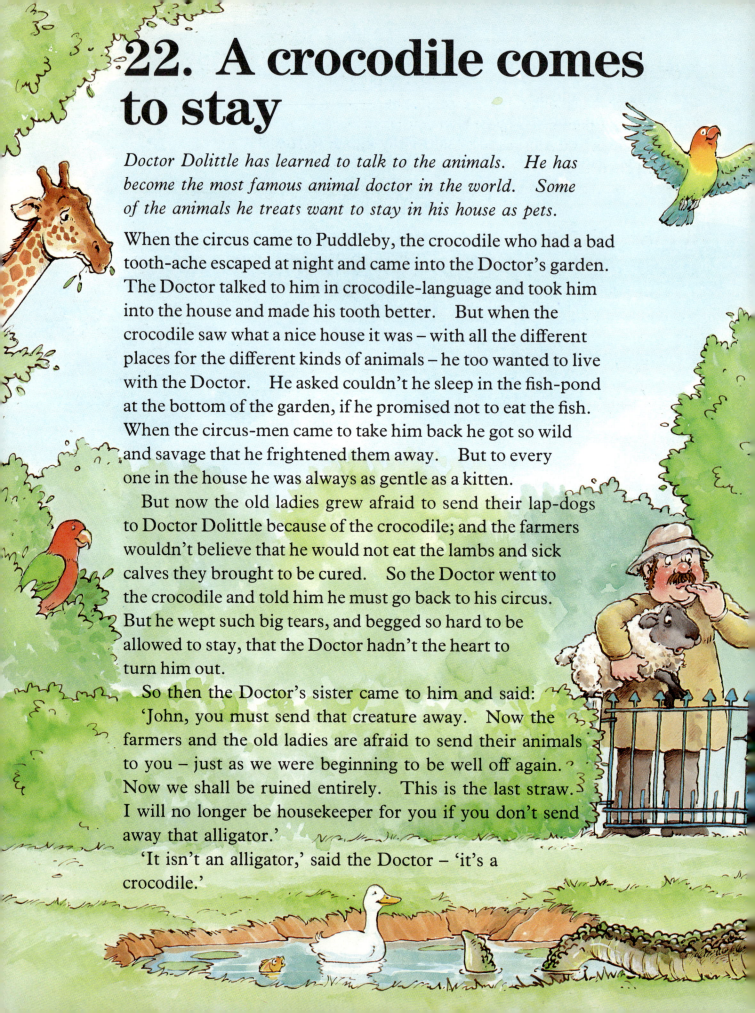

Doctor Dolittle has learned to talk to the animals.   He has become the most famous animal doctor in the world.   Some of the animals he treats want to stay in his house as pets.

When the circus came to Puddleby, the crocodile who had a bad tooth-ache escaped at night and came into the Doctor's garden. The Doctor talked to him in crocodile-language and took him into the house and made his tooth better.   But when the crocodile saw what a nice house it was – with all the different places for the different kinds of animals – he too wanted to live with the Doctor.   He asked couldn't he sleep in the fish-pond at the bottom of the garden, if he promised not to eat the fish. When the circus-men came to take him back he got so wild and savage that he frightened them away.   But to every one in the house he was always as gentle as a kitten.

But now the old ladies grew afraid to send their lap-dogs to Doctor Dolittle because of the crocodile; and the farmers wouldn't believe that he would not eat the lambs and sick calves they brought to be cured.   So the Doctor went to the crocodile and told him he must go back to his circus. But he wept such big tears, and begged so hard to be allowed to stay, that the Doctor hadn't the heart to turn him out.

So then the Doctor's sister came to him and said:

'John, you must send that creature away.   Now the farmers and the old ladies are afraid to send their animals to you – just as we were beginning to be well off again. Now we shall be ruined entirely.   This is the last straw. I will no longer be housekeeper for you if you don't send away that alligator.'

'It isn't an alligator,' said the Doctor – 'it's a crocodile.'

Key points

1. Why did the crocodile go to Doctor Dolittle's house?
2. Why did it decide to stay with Doctor Dolittle?
3. How did the crocodile prove it was a well-behaved crocodile?
4. What did the farmers and old ladies think about the crocodile?
5. Why was Doctor Dolittle's sister so worried about it?

A closer look

Imagine you were Doctor Dolittle, and you had to decide whether to keep the crocodile or not.   What were the reasons for keeping it and what were the reasons for sending it back to the circus?

For talk

Do you think the farmers and old ladies were right to be afraid of the crocodile? Talk about other animals that have a bad reputation, like wolves, snakes and sharks.   Do you think we should be afraid of them?

For writing

The crocodile had different moods.   It was gentle with the people in the house but fierce with the men from the circus. Write about *your* moods and the times when they change.

Read on

What will Doctor Dolittle do with the crocodile?   What will happen when he gets a message from Africa to say the monkeys are ill?   Read *The Story of Doctor Dolittle* by Hugh Lofting.

23. A shock for the robbers

*Granny Smith has suddenly turned into a Super Gran.
She has super-strength, super-speed, super-sight and
super-everything. Even when she is on the bus, she
can see through the walls of a bank.*

Just as the Capitol Bank opened its doors after lunch,
three bank-robbers with stocking-masks over their faces
forced their way in and slammed the door shut behind
them. Outside, in a getaway car, they left a fourth man,
waiting for them. The leader stood in front of the counter,
pointing a gun at the bank staff, while, behind the counter,
his two mates filled sacks with money from a large safe.

'Hurry up, Harry, Joe,' he urged, as he waved
his gun towards the manager and his staff.
'Don't take all day . . . .'

But that was about as far as the bank-robbers got!

Suddenly, there was a terrific bang from the front of
the bank as the door shattered and Super Gran hurtled
her way through the hole she'd made in it – making a
sudden, and dramatic, entrance!

The leader swung his head round and his mouth gaped
open, in amazement, when he saw that a little old lady
was responsible for the big jagged hole in the door. It was
a big enough shock to see *anyone* come hurtling through a
hole kicked in a big, thick door, but a little old lady . . . whew!

But that was all the leader saw. For that was all he
had time to see! Super Gran hit him once, before he
could move or aim his gun at her, or do anything. He
slumped to the floor and lay there, suddenly desiring a
long, deep sleep!

56

Super Gran didn't stop.   She leapt over the fallen crook and vaulted nimbly over the bank counter – steel grille and all! – and landed beside Harry and Joe, who'd stopped filling the sacks when they heard the door being shattered and saw their boss being battered!   And now it was their turn!

Key points

1. What did the bank-robbers do inside the bank?
2. How did they plan to escape from the bank?
3. Why did they think nobody else could get into the bank?
4. How did Super Gran get in?
5. How did she deal with the leader of the robbers?

A closer look

Imagine you were in the bank when the robbery began.   Write down what you told the police, when they asked you what you saw.

For talk

Robbers steal from houses, shops and flats as well as banks. Talk about ways people can guard their homes and property.

For writing

You have now met Super Gran and her amazing powers. Imagine she had another adventure on her way home. Write a story about it.

Read on

How did Granny Smith turn into Super Gran? You can read how it happened and about all her adventures in *Super Gran* by Forrest Wilson.

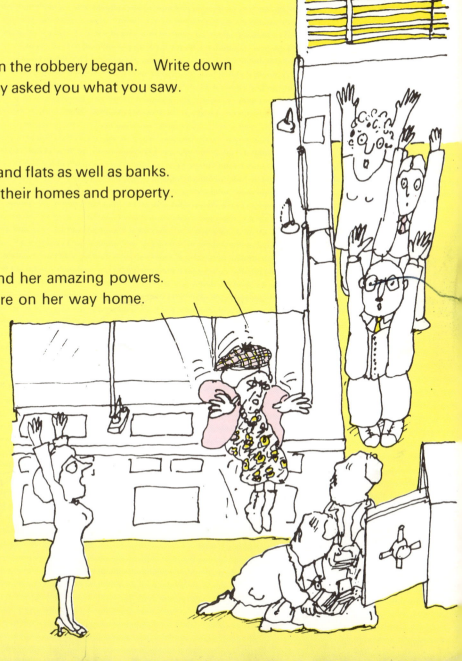

24. An elephant's revenge

The hunters of the village of Gwelo have killed Samburu, the giant elephant. That night, the whole village is woken up by a great noise.

In the flickering light of the torches the men suddenly caught sight of an enormous figure rampaging through their crops. They could see the glinting tusks of an elephant. Its mighty trunk snaked out and seized a sheaf of maize stems, thrust it into its mouth and then tore out another cluster by the roots.

All at once the elephant turned towards the men. Its eyes gleamed redly. Its huge tusks glinted menacingly. It raised its trunk and trumpeted again.

'Flee!' cried Bongang, and as he was headman of the village he always liked to set an example, so he was the first to flee. 'It is the ghost of Samburu! Flee for your lives! The spirit of the elephant has returned to take vengeance on us! Run for your lives!'

And the entire village fled from that fearful visitor! The women gathered up the totos in their arms, the grandmothers seized the older children by the hand, the dogs ran yelping at their heels, while in front of everybody ran the men. The people of Gwelo hid trembling in the forest while the elephant continued his fearful work. He trampled the crops, broke down many

banana trees, ate up all the yams. Then he entered the deserted village and barged over some of the mud huts, stripped the thatch from the roofs and smashed up the canoes by the riverside.

Key points

1. How were the villagers able to see the elephant in the night?
2. Why did Bongang tell them to flee for their lives?
3. What else do you think made them run away?
4. Why do you think the men fled in front of the women and children?
5. Where did the villagers go?

A closer look

Imagine you were one of the village children. When you were much older, you told your own children what the elephant looked like and what you saw that night. Write down what you said.

For talk

Talk about times when *you* have run away from someone or something.

For writing

For this piece of writing you need a picture of an animal. Look closely at your picture and then write an interesting description of the animal.

Read on

Has the ghost of Samburu returned to the village? What will the people of Gwelo do? Read *The Ghost Elephant* by Alan C. Jenkins, a story full of mystery and danger in Africa.

25. Wind and darkness

It is a dark and windy night in March. Mr Pennyquick has been painting signs in the funfair at the end of the pier. His young friend, Davy, has been helping him. Suddenly, Mr Pennyquick falls from his ladder and is lying unconscious. Davy knows he has to go back down the pier to get help. But the pier is completely dark and Mr Pennyquick's torch was broken in his fall.

Davy slid out of the door and was engulfed by the noise. Everything roaring with wind. Everything black and wet and hissing and splashing. It blew through his thin sweater as he stood there, frozen in the little pool of yellow from the light behind him.

'Just a walk down the pier, a walk down the pier,' he told himself as he shivered.

He wished he had his anorak. But then, if he was going to start wishing he might as well wish for something worthwhile. Like a torch. Like somebody coming out of the darkness to help him. Like closing his eyes and turning the clock back and not having this happen at all.

The rain splattered over him, chilling his bones until he felt like the skeleton Mr Pennyquick had been painting, shaking and exposed. The wet got in his eyes and down his shirt and into his shoes. It plastered his hair down round his collar and over his face.

Still he did not move. Outside the pool of light was no-man's-land. Different to the daylight when it was just a walk down the pier with deckchairs and people fishing.

'You certainly have an imagination, Davy,' Mr Pennyquick had said often.

'Those pictures of yours – all nightmares and creepy crawlies,' Meg had said.

Too much imagination, Davy thought.   Like now, when the
pier wasn't a pier any more but a dark tunnel with fingers
reaching out as you walked and noises and splashing and . . .

Davy shut his eyes.   This was no good.   He had to close
his mind up, put the lid down and sit on it – at least until
he reached the other end of the pier.   Come on, feet – *move*.
Out of the yellow and into the black and don't stop!

It was difficult to know where to walk.   In the centre
of the pier the wind buffeted him until he could hardly
stand.   Without anything to hold on to he began losing
his sense of direction.   Was he still going forwards or sideways?

Somehow he found his way over to the rail at the
side.   It was better at first, moving hand over hand, but
then the sea splashed up over his feet and legs and he
became frightened he would be washed over the side.

He looked back to the light from the doors of the
funfair.   How far had he come, ten, twenty miles?   It
seemed at least that far but the light told him different,
he was barely half-way.

Then he heard the crash.

Key points

1. Where was the only light on the pier?
2. Why was it so hard to walk down the pier?
3. Why do you think Davy tried to find the rail at the side of the pier?
4. Why did the rail seem a dangerous place to be?
5. Where was Davy when he heard the crash?

A closer look

A. Both Mr Pennyquick and Meg, his grand-daughter, said Davy had a vivid imagination.   The passage tells you what Davy was thinking when he was on the pier.   Write down what he was thinking at each of these times.   Then check to see if you were right.
   1. When he went out of the door of the funfair;
   2. When he stood there and shivered;
   3. When he wished he had his anorak;
   4. When he felt the rain;
   5. When he remembered the pier in daylight;
   6. When he remembered what Meg said about his pictures;
   7. When he looked down the pier into the darkness;
   8. When the sea splashed over this legs;
   9. When he looked back at the light in the funfair;
   10. When he heard the crash.

B. Using *only* what you have learned from the passage and the picture write a short description of the pier *in the daylight*.

For talk

Davy had to get help for Mr Pennyquick.   Talk about the problems he faced and what you would have done if you had been Davy.

GALE WARNING

The wind breaks bound, tossing the oak and chestnut,
Whirling the paper at street corners,
The city clerks are harassed, wrestling head-down:
The gulls are blown inland.

Three slates fall from a roof,
The promenade is in danger:
Inland, the summer fête is postponed,
The British glider record broken.

The wind blows through the city, cleansing,
Whipping the posters from the hoardings,
Tearing the bunting and the banners,
The wind blows steadily, and as it will.

Michael Roberts

For writing

Both the passage and the poem describe a strong wind. Write about a windy day
you remember and what it felt like when you were outside, in the wind.

Read on

Will Davy be able to reach the entrance to the pier and get help?
What has caused the crash he has just heard?   Read the exciting story
A Walk down the Pier by John Escott.

Book List

Joan Aiken   *A Necklace of Raindrops and other stories*
Phyllis Arkle   *Two Village Dinosaurs*
Elizabeth Beresford   *Wombling Free*
Michael Bond   *Here Comes Thursday!*
Lucy Boston   *The Castle of Yew*
Petronella Breinburg   *Brinsly's Dream*
Diana Carter   *Zozu the Robot*
Dick Cate   *Old Dog, New Tricks*
Helen Clare   *Five Dolls in a House*
Roald Dahl   *The Magic Finger*
John Escott   *A Walk Down the Pier*
Anita Feagles   *Casey the Utterly Impossible Horse*
Nina Warner Hooke   *The Snow Kitten*
Alan C Jenkins   *The Ghost Elephant*
Hugh Lofting   *The Story of Doctor Dolittle*
Barbara Sleigh   *Ninety-nine Dragons*
Catherine Storr   *Clever Polly and the Stupid Wolf*
David Thomson   *Danny Fox*
Barbara Euphan Todd   *Worzel Gummidge Again*
Jill Tomlinson   *The Owl who was Afraid of the Dark*
Teresa Verschoyle   *Matthew's Secret Surprises*
Jan Wahl   *Pleasant Fieldmouse*
Ursula Moray Williams   *Adventures of the Little Wooden Horse*
Jean Wills   *The Sawdust Secret*
Forrest Wilson   *Super Gran*

Acknowledgments

The author and publishers wish to thank the following for permission to use extracts from copyright material in this publication: George Allen and Unwin for *The Magic Finger* by Roald Dahl, illustrations by Pat Marriott; Ernest Benn Ltd for *Wombling Free* by Elisabeth Beresford, illustrations by Edgar Hodges; The Bodley Head for *The Castle of Yew* by Lucy Boston, illustration by Margery Gill, and for *Five Dolls in a House* by Helen Clare; Burke Publishing Co Ltd for *Brinsly's Dream* by Petronella Breinburg, illustration by Robert Hales; Jonathan Cape Ltd for an illustration by Jan Pienkowski from *A Necklace of Raindrops*; Faber and Faber Publishers for 'Gale Warning' from *Collected Poems* by Michael Roberts, and for *Clever Polly and the Stupid Wolf* by Catherine Storr; Victor Gollancz Ltd for *Casey the Utterly Impossible Horse* by Anita Feagles, illustration by Roger Smith; Granada Publishing Ltd for 'Neighbours' from *Daybreak* by Leonard Clark, and for 'The Wendigo' from *Funny Poems* by Ogden Nash (ed. Deborah Manley); Hamish Hamilton Ltd for *Old Dogs New Tricks* © Dick Cate 1978 illustration © Trevor Stubley 1978, and for *The Sawdust Secret* © Jean Wills 1973, and for *A Walk Down The Pier* © John Escott 1977 black and white illustration © Frances Phillips 1977; Harrap Ltd for *Adventures of the Little Wooden Horse* by Ursula Moray Williams, illustration by Peggy Fortnum, and for *Here Comes Thursday!* by Michael Bond, illustration by Daphne Rowles; A M Heath and Co Ltd and the Estate of Barbara Euphan Todd for *Worzel Gummidge Again*, and for *A Necklace of Raindrops* by Joan Aiken published by Jonathan Cape Ltd; Hodder and Stoughton Ltd for *Ninety-nine Dragons* by Barbara Sleigh, and for *Two Village Dinosaurs* by Phyllis Arkle; William Heinemann Ltd for *Pleasant Field-mouse* by Jan Wahl, illustration by Maurice Sendak, reprinted by permission of Worlds Work Ltd; Methuen Children's Books for *The Owl Who Was Afraid of the Dark* by Jill Tomlinson, illustration by Joanne Cole; Penguin Books Ltd for *Matthew's Secret Surprises* by Teresa Verschoyle © Teresa Wills (Puffin Books 1979, pp 20–22), and for *The Snow Kitten* © Nina Warner Hooke, illustration © Gavin Rowe (Puffin Books 1978, pp 82–83 and frontispiece), and for *Danny Fox* © David Thomson, illustration by Gunvor Edwards (Puffin Books 1966, pp 14–18), and for *The Ghost Elephant* © Alan C Jenkins, illustration © Nelda Prins (Puffin Books 1981, pp 31–33); Estate of James Reeves for 'The Black Pebble' by James Reeves © 1952 from his *Complete Poems for Children*; Sidgwick and Jackson Ltd for *Zozu the Robot* by Diana Carter, illustration by Mike Rose, and for 'Four and Eight' by ffrida Wolfe from *The Very Thing*; Ralph M Vicinanza for *The Story of Doctor Dolittle* by Hugh Lofting, first published in the U K by Jonathan Cape Ltd 1922. The specially commissioned illustrations are by Michael Charlton, Robert Geary, Annabel Large, Steve Smallman and Frances Thatcher.